Y0-DKN-995

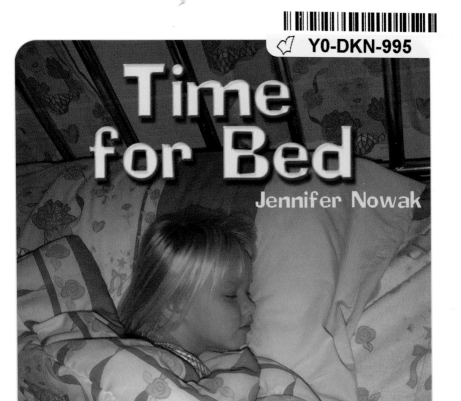

Time for Bed

Jennifer Nowak

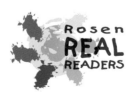

Rosen Classroom Books and Materials
New York

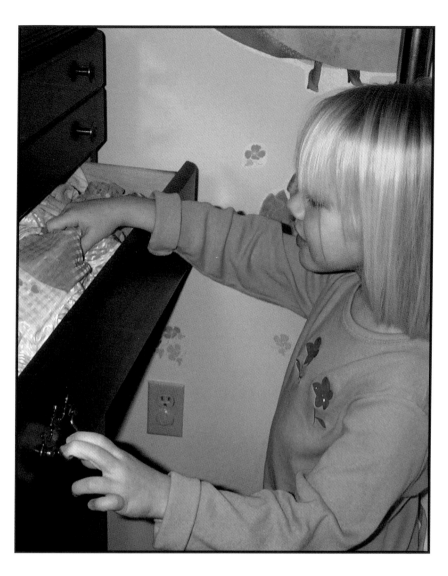

It is time for bed.

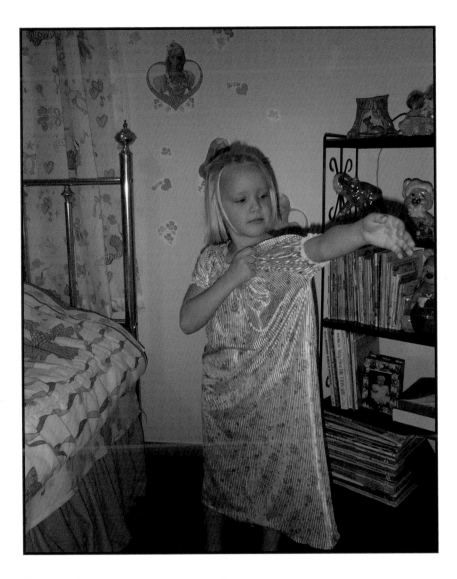

I put on my pajamas.

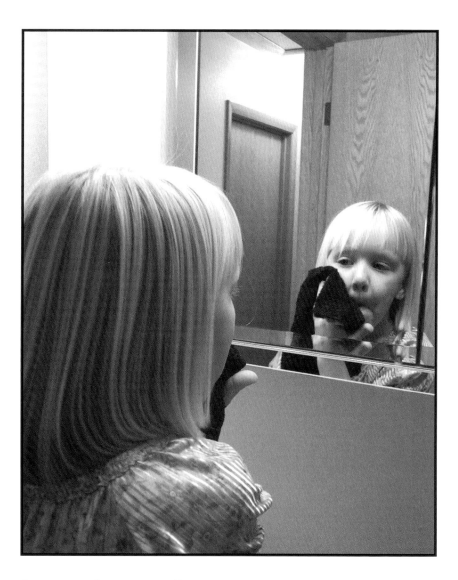

I wash my face.

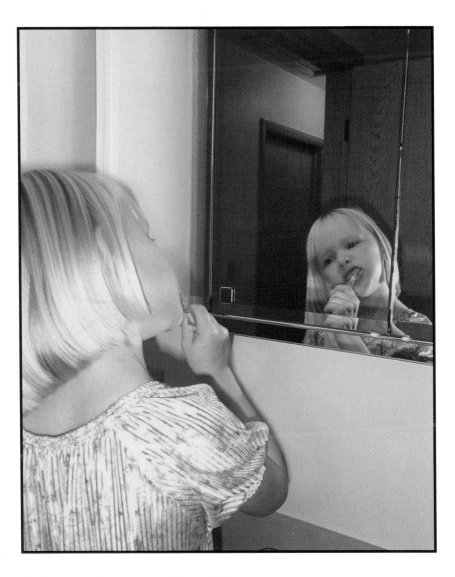

I brush my teeth.

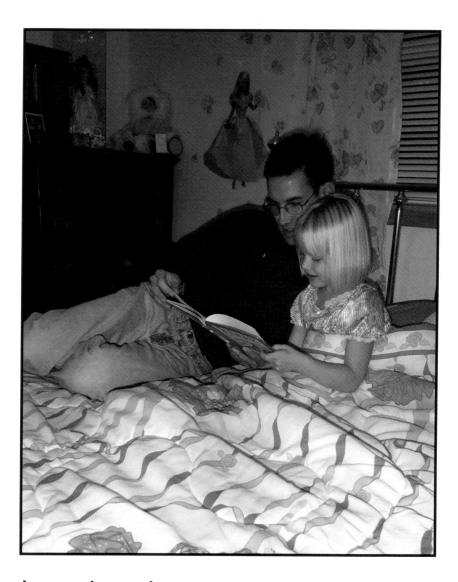

I read a story.

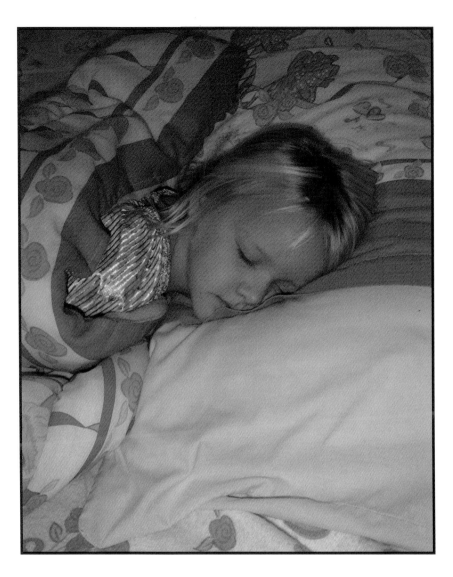

Then I go to sleep.

Words to Know

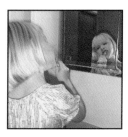

brush

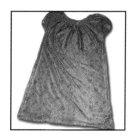

pajamas

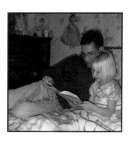

read

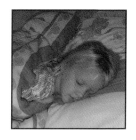

sleep

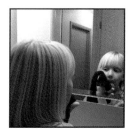

wash